PIANO · VOCAL · GUITAR

THE GRAMMY AWARDS®

SONG OF THE YEAR

1958 – 1969

GRAMMY, GRAMMY Awards and the gramophone logo are registered
trademarks of The Recording Academy® and are used under license.

Visit The Recording Academy Online at
www.grammy.com

ISBN 978-1-4584-1557-8

HAL•LEONARD®
CORPORATION
7777 W. BLUEMOUND RD. P.O. BOX 13819 MILWAUKEE, WI 53213

Visit Hal Leonard Online at
www.halleonard.com

>> Adele at the 54th GRAMMY Awards

THE RECORDING ACADEMY®

When it comes to music on TV, the last few years alone have seen some very memorable moments: Paul McCartney, Bruce Springsteen, Dave Grohl, and Joe Walsh jamming on "The End" from the Beatles' classic *Abbey Road*; Adele making her triumphant first live singing appearance after throat surgery to perform "Rolling In The Deep"; Pink dripping wet and hovering 20 feet above the stage while singing a note-perfect version of "Glitter In The Air"; and Lady Gaga hatching from a massive egg to perform "Born This Way." All of these performances, and many more, took place on the famed GRAMMY Awards® stage.

The GRAMMY® Award is indisputedly the most sought-after recognition of excellence in recorded music worldwide. Over more than half a century, the GRAMMY Awards have become both music's biggest honor and Music's Biggest Night®, with the annual telecast drawing tens of millions of viewers nationwide and millions more internationally.

And with evolving categories that always reflect important current artistic waves — such as dance/electronica music — as well as setting a record for social TV engagement in 2012, the GRAMMYs keep moving forward, serving as a real-time barometer of music's cultural impact.

The Recording Academy is the organization that produces the GRAMMY Awards. Consisting of the artists, musicians, songwriters, producers, engineers, and other professionals who make the music you enjoy every day on the radio, your streaming or download services, or in the concert hall, The Academy is a dynamic institution with an active agenda aimed at supporting and nurturing music and the people who make it.

Whether it's joining with recording artists to ensure their creative rights are protected, providing ongoing professional development services to the recording community or supporting the health and well-being of music creators and music education in our schools, The Recording Academy has become the recording industry's primary organization for professional and educational outreach, human services, arts advocacy, and cultural enrichment.

The Academy represents members from all corners of the professional music world — from the biggest recording stars to unsung music educators — all brought together under the banner of building a better creative environment for music and its makers.

» Paul McCartney at the 2012 MusiCares Person of the Year gala in his honor

Christopher Polk/WireImage.com

» Trombone Shorty and Mavis Staples at the GRAMMY Foundation's Music Preservation Project event in 2012

Michael Kovac/WireImage.com

MUSICARES FOUNDATION®

MusiCares® was established by The Recording Academy to provide a safety net of critical assistance for music people in times of need. MusiCares has developed into a premier support system for music people, providing resources to cover a wide range of financial, medical and personal emergencies through innovative programs and services, including regular eBay auctions of one-of-a-kind memorabilia that are open to the public. The charity has been supported by the contributions and participation of artists such as Neil Diamond, Aretha Franklin, Paul McCartney, Bruce Springsteen, Barbra Streisand, and Neil Young — just to name the organization's most recent annual Person of the Year fundraiser honorees — and so many others through the years.

THE GRAMMY FOUNDATION®

The GRAMMY Foundation's mission is to cultivate the understanding, appreciation and advancement of the contribution of recorded music to American culture. The Foundation accomplishes this mission through programs and activities designed to engage the music industry and cultural community as well as the general public. The Foundation works to bring national attention to important issues such as the value and impact of music and arts education and the urgency of preserving our rich cultural legacy, and it accomplishes this work by engaging music professionals — from big-name stars to working professionals and educators — to work directly with students.

» Secretary of the Department of Health and Human Services Kathleen Sebelius and Recording Academy President/CEO Neil Portnow present the Recording Artists' Coalition Award to John Mayer at the GRAMMYs on the Hill Awards in Washington, D.C., in 2012

Paul Morigi/WireImage.com

» The GRAMMY Museum in downtown Los Angeles

Courtesy of the GRAMMY Museum

FIGHTING FOR MUSICIANS' RIGHTS

Over the last 15 years, The Recording Academy has built a presence in the nation's capital, working to amplify the voice of music creators in national policy matters. Today, called the "supersized musicians lobby" by *Congressional Quarterly*, The Academy's Advocacy & Industry Relations office in Washington, D.C., is the leading representative of the collective world of recording professionals — artists, songwriters, producers, and engineers — through its GRAMMYs on the Hill® Initiative. The Academy has taken a leadership role in the fight to expand radio performance royalties to all music creators, worked on behalf of musicians on censorship concerns and regularly supported musicians on legislative issues that impact the vitality of music.

THE GRAMMY MUSEUM®

Since opening its doors in December 2008, the GRAMMY Museum has served as a dynamic educational and interactive institution dedicated to the power of music. The four-story, 30,000-square foot facility is part of L.A. Live, the premier sports and entertainment destination in downtown Los Angeles. The Museum serves the community with interactive, permanent and traveling exhibits and an array of public and education programs. We invite you to visit us when you're in the Los Angeles area.

As you can see, The Recording Academy is so much more than the annual GRAMMY telecast once a year, even if that one show is Music's Biggest Night. To keep up with all The Academy's activities, visit GRAMMY.com regularly, and join the conversation on our social networks:

 Facebook.com/TheGRAMMYs

 Twitter.com/TheGRAMMYs

 YouTube.com/TheGRAMMYs

 TheGRAMMYs.tumblr.com

 Foursquare.com/TheGRAMMYs

 Instagram (user name: TheGRAMMYs)

Google+ (gplus.to/TheGRAMMYs)

TABLE OF CONTENTS (ALPHABETICAL)

TABLE OF CONTENTS (CHRONOLOGICAL)

🏆 WINNER

AS LONG AS HE NEEDS ME

from the Broadway Musical OLIVER!

Words & Music by
LIONEL BART

BATTLE OF NEW ORLEANS

Words and Music by
JIMMY DRIFTWOOD

Moderately, like a march

In

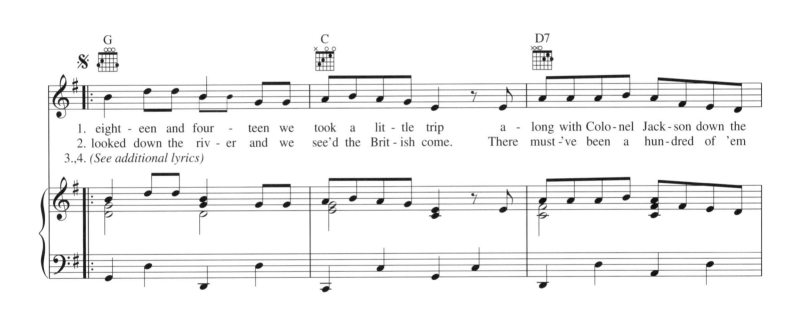

1. eight - een and four - teen we took a lit - tle trip a - long with Colo - nel Jack - son down the
2. looked down the riv - er and we see'd the Brit - ish come. There must - 've been a hun - dred of 'em
3., 4. (See additional lyrics)

might - y Mis - sis - sip'. We took a lit - tle ba - con and we took a lit - tle beans and we
beat - in' on the drum. They stepped so high and they made their bu - gles ring, while we

Additional Lyrics

3. Old Hick'ry said we could take 'em by surprise
   If we didn't fire a musket till we looked 'em in the eyes.
   We held our fire till we see'd their faces well,
   Then we opened up our squirrel guns and really gave 'em hell.
   Chorus

4. We fired our cannon till the barrel melted down,
   So we grabbed an alligator and we fought another round.
   We filled his head with cannon balls and powdered his behind;
   And when we touched the powder off, the 'gator lost his mind.
   Chorus

BY THE TIME I GET TO PHOENIX

Words and Music by
JIMMY WEBB

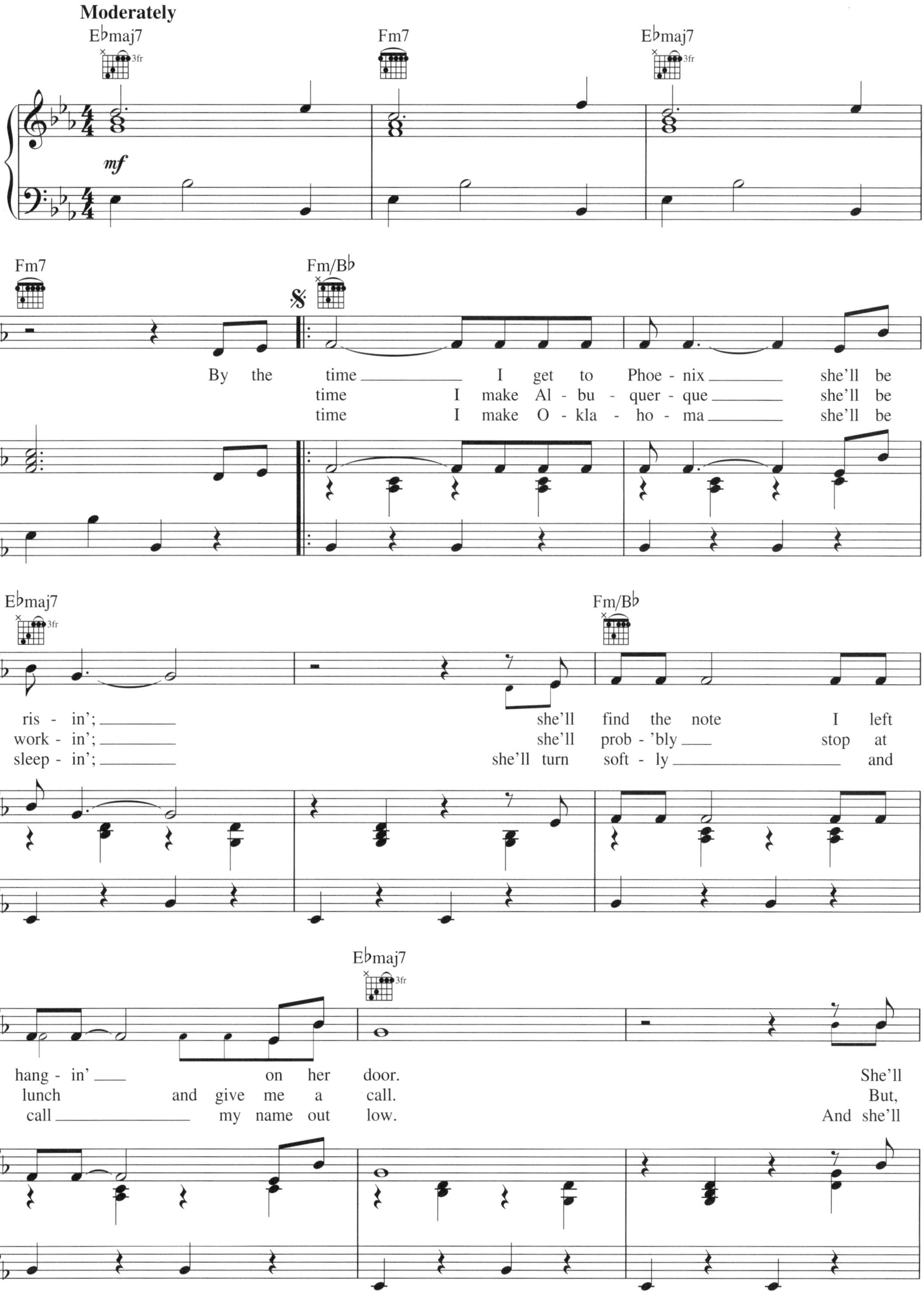

Moderately
E♭maj7
Fm7
E♭maj7
mf
Fm7
Fm/B♭
By the time I get to Phoe - nix she'll be
time I make Al - bu - quer - que she'll be
time I make O - kla - ho - ma she'll be
E♭maj7
Fm/B♭
ris - in'; she'll find the note I left
work - in'; she'll prob - 'bly stop at
sleep - in'; she'll turn soft - ly and
E♭maj7
hang - in' on her door. She'll
lunch and give me a call. But,
call my name out low. And she'll

BIG BAD JOHN

Words and Music by
JIMMY DEAN

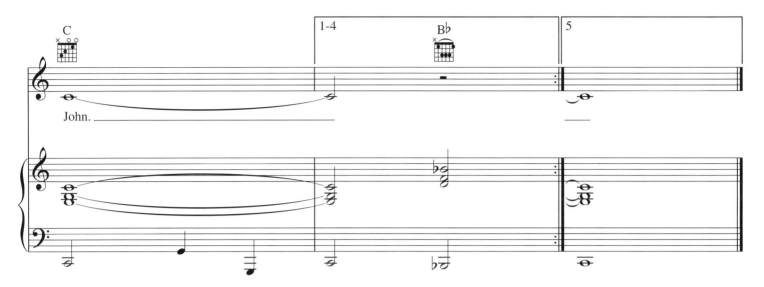

Verses

1. Every morning at the mine you could see him arrive,
   He stood six-foot-six and weighed two-forty-five.
   Kind of broad at the shoulder and narrow at the hip,
   And everybody knew you didn't give no lip to Big John!
   Refrain

2. Nobody seemed to know where John called home,
   He just drifted into town and stayed all alone.
   He didn't say much, a-kinda quiet and shy,
   And if you spoke at all, you just said, "Hi" to Big John!
   Somebody said he came from New Orleans,
   Where he got in a fight over a Cajun queen.
   And a crashing blow from a huge right hand
   Sent a Louisiana fellow to the promised land. Big John!
   Refrain

3. Then came the day at the bottom of the mine
   When a timber cracked and the men started crying.
   Miners were praying and hearts beat fast,
   And everybody thought that they'd breathed their last 'cept John.
   Through the dust and the smoke of this man-made hell
   Walked a giant of a man that the miners knew well.
   Grabbed a sagging timber and gave out with a groan,
   And, like a giant oak tree, just stood there alone. Big John!
   Refrain

4. And with all of his strength, he gave a mighty shove;
   Then a miner yelled out, "There's a light up above!"
   And twenty men scrambled from a would-be grave,
   And now there's only one left down there to save; Big John!
   With jacks and timbers they started back down
   Then came that rumble way down in the ground,
   And smoke and gas belched out of that mine,
   Everybody knew it was the end of the line for Big John!
   Refrain

5. Now they never re-opened that worthless pit,
   They just placed a marble stand in front of it;
   These few words are written on that stand:
   "At the bottom of this mine lies a big, big man; Big John!"
   Refrain

BORN FREE
from the Columbia Pictures' Release BORN FREE

Words by DON BLACK
Music by JOHN BARRY

Born free, _____ as free as the wind blows, _____ as free as the
Live free, _____ and beau-ty sur-rounds you, _____ the world still a-

grass grows, born free to fol-low your heart.
stounds you, born each

time you look at a star. _____

CALL ME IRRESPONSIBLE
from the Paramount Picture PAPA'S DELICATE CONDITION

Words by SAMMY CAHN
Music by JAMES VAN HEUSEN

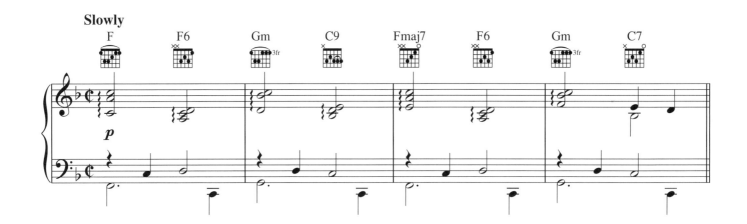

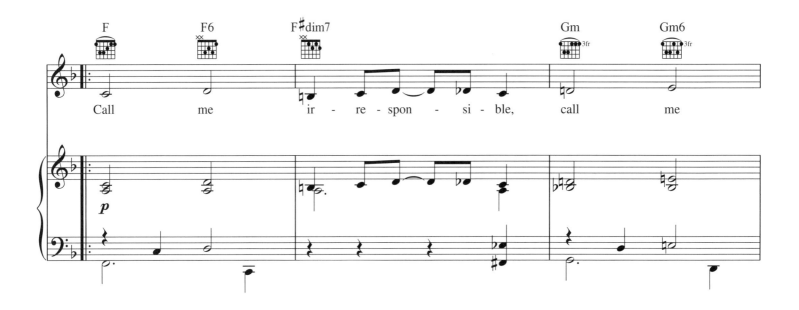

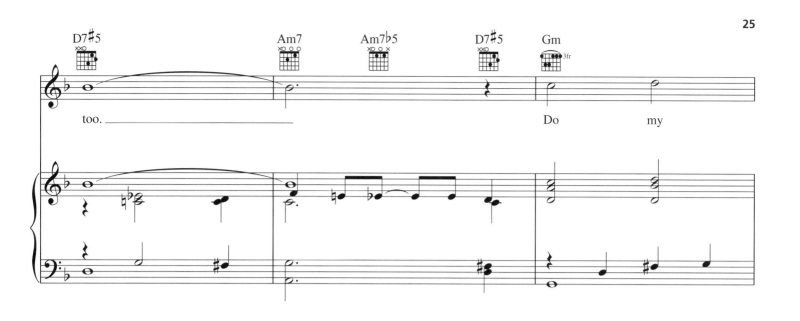

too. _____ Do my

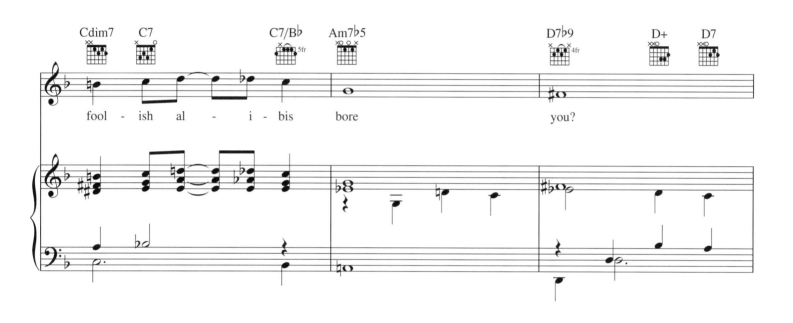

fool - ish al - i - bis bore you?

Well, I'm not too clev - er. I just a -

CATCH A FALLING STAR

Words and Music by PAUL VANCE
and LEE POCKRISS

DEAR HEART
Theme from the Film DEAR HEART

Music by HENRY MANCINI
Words by JAY LIVINGSTON and RAY EVANS

DAYS OF WINE AND ROSES

Theme from the Film DAYS OF WINE AND ROSES

Lyric by JOHNNY MERCER
Music by HENRY MANCINI

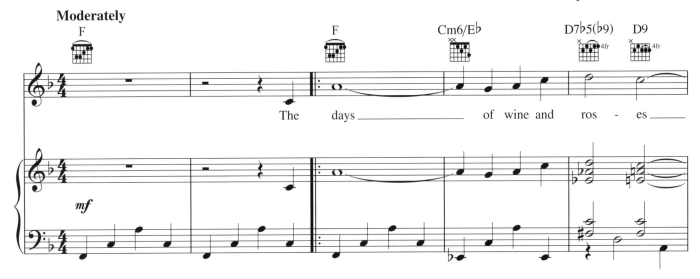

THE EXODUS SONG

from EXODUS

Words by PAT BOONE
Music by ERNEST GOLD

FEVER

Words and Music by JOHN DAVENPORT
and EDDIE COOLEY

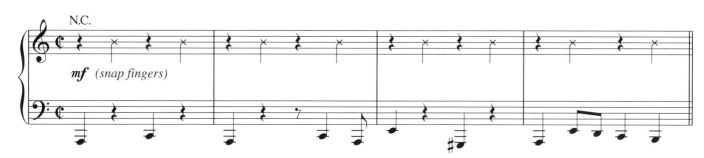

1. Nev - er know how much I love you, nev - er know how much I
2. Sun lights up the day - time, moon lights up the night.
3. Ro - me - o loved Ju - li - et. Ju - li - et, she felt the
4. Cap - tain Smith and Po - ca - hon - tas had a ver - y mad af -
5. Now you've lis - tened to my sto - ry. Here's the point that I have

care. When you put your arms a - round me, I get a
night. I light up when you call my name, and you
same. When he put his arms a - round her, he said,
fair. When her dad - dy tried to kill him, she said,
made. Chicks were born to give you fe - ver, be it

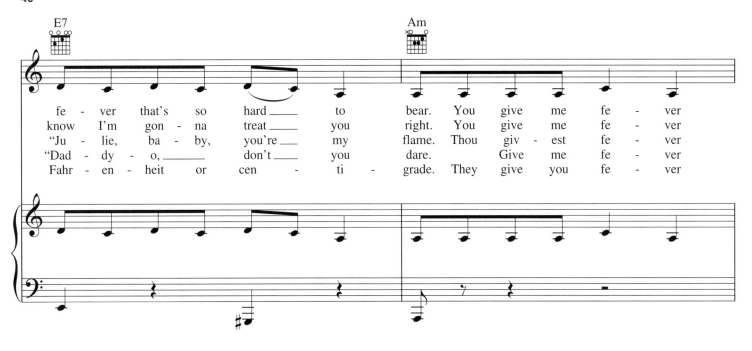

fe - ver that's so hard ____ to bear. You give me fe - ver
know I'm gon - na treat ____ you right. You give me fe - ver
"Ju - lie, ba - by, you're ____ my flame. Thou giv - est fe - ver
"Dad - dy - o, ____ don't ____ you dare. Give me fe - ver
Fahr - en - heit or cen - ti - grade. They give you fe - ver

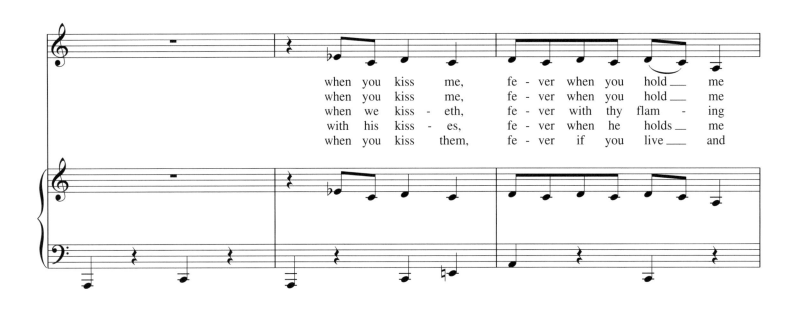

when you kiss me, fe - ver when you hold ____ me
when you kiss me, fe - ver when you hold ____ me
when we kiss - eth, fe - ver with thy flam - ing
with his kiss - es, fe - ver when he holds ____ me
when you kiss them, fe - ver if you live ____ and

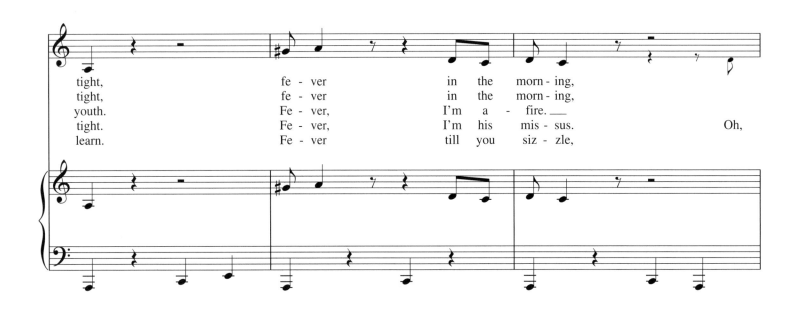

tight, fe - ver in the morn - ing,
tight, fe - ver in the morn - ing,
youth. Fe - ver, I'm a - fire. ____
tight. Fe - ver, I'm his mis - sus. Oh,
learn. Fe - ver till you siz - zle,

GAMES PEOPLE PLAY

Words and Music by
JOE SOUND

GENTLE ON MY MIND

Words and Music by
JOHN HARTFORD

1. It's know-ing that your door is al-ways o-pen and your
2.-4. *(See additional lyrics)*

path is free to walk that

makes me tend to leave my sleep-ing bag rolled up and stashed be-hind your

riv - ers of my mem-'ry that keeps you ev - er gen - tle on my

mind.

It's

mind.

Additional Lyrics

2. It's not clinging to the rocks and ivy planted on their columns now that binds me,
Or something that somebody said because they thought we fit together walkin'.
It's just knowing that the world will not be cursing or forgiving when I walk along
Some railroad track and find
That you're moving on the backroads by the rivers of my memory, and for hours
You're just gentle on my mind.

3. Though the wheat fields and the clotheslines and junkyards and the highways
Come between us,
And some other woman crying to her mother 'cause she turned and I was gone.
I still run in silence, tears of joy might stain my face and summer sun might
Burn me 'til I'm blind,
But not to where I cannot see you walkin' on the backroads by the rivers flowing
Gentle on my mind.

4. I dip my cup of soup back from the gurglin' cracklin' caldron in some train yard,
My beard a roughening coal pile and a dirty hat pulled low across my face.
Through cupped hands 'round a tin can I pretend I hold you to my breast and find
That you're waving from the backroads by the rivers of my memory, ever smilin',
Ever gentle on my mind.

GIGI
from GIGI

Words by ALAN JAY LERNER
Music by FREDERICK LOEWE

THE GOOD LIFE

Words by JACK REARDON and JEAN BROUSSOLLE
Music by SACHA DISTEL

Oh, the good life _____ full of fun ____ seems to be ____ the i-

deal. _____ Yes, the good life _____ lets you

hide ____ all the sad - ness you feel. _____ You won't

A HARD DAY'S NIGHT

Words and Music by JOHN LENNON
and PAUL McCARTNEY

Moderately, with a beat

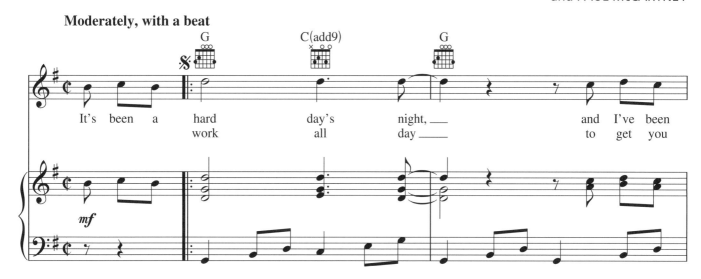

It's been a hard day's night, ___ and I've been
work all day ___ to get you

work-ing like a dog. ___ It's been a hard day's night, ___
mon - ey to buy your things. ___ And it's worth it just to hear you say ___

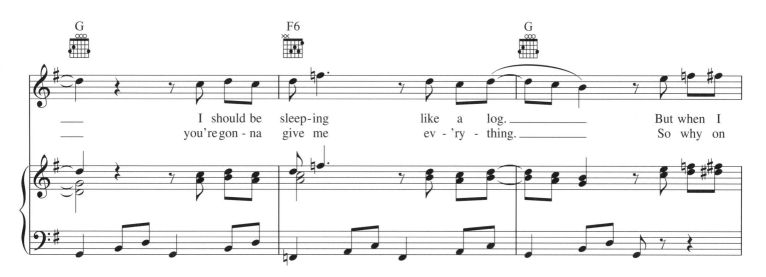

I should be sleep-ing like a log. ___ But when I
you're gon - na give me ev - 'ry - thing. ___ So why on

HARPER VALLEY P.T.A.

Words and Music by
TOM T. HALL

HE'LL HAVE TO GO

Words and Music by JOE ALLISON
and AUDREY ALLISON

Moderately

HELLO, DOLLY!

from HELLO, DOLLY!

Music and Lyric by
JERRY HERMAN

HIGH HOPES

Words by SAMMY CAHN
Music by JAMES VAN HEUSEN

HEY JUDE

Words and Music by JOHN LENNON
and PAUL McCARTNEY

HONEY

Words and Music by
BOBBY RUSSELL

Moderately

See the tree how big it's grown, but friend, it has-n't been too long it was-n't big.
She was al-ways young at heart, _ kind-a dumb and kind-a smart, and I loved her so.

I laughed at her and she got mad, the first day that she plant-ed it was
I sur-prised her with a pup-py, kept me up all Christ-mas eve, two

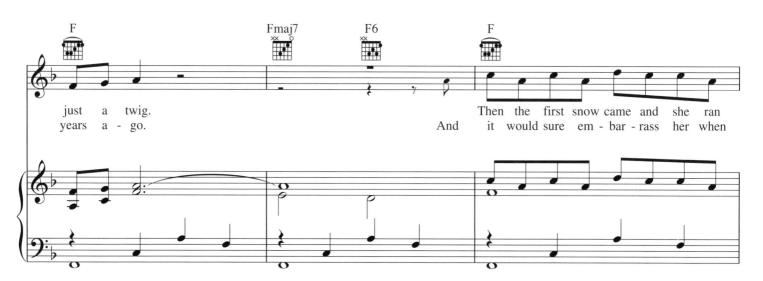

just a twig.
years a-go.

Then the first snow came and she ran
And it would sure em-bar-rass her when

I KNOW

Words and Music by EDITH LINDEMAN
and CARL STUTZ

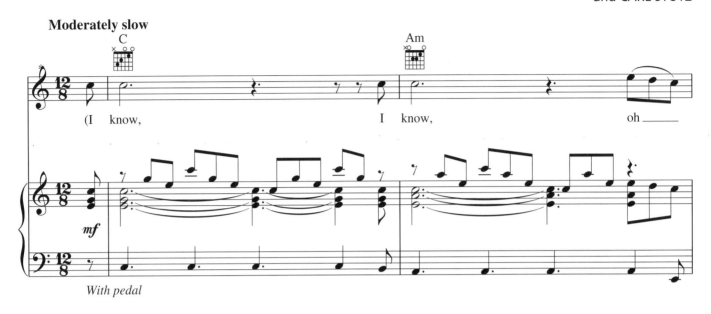

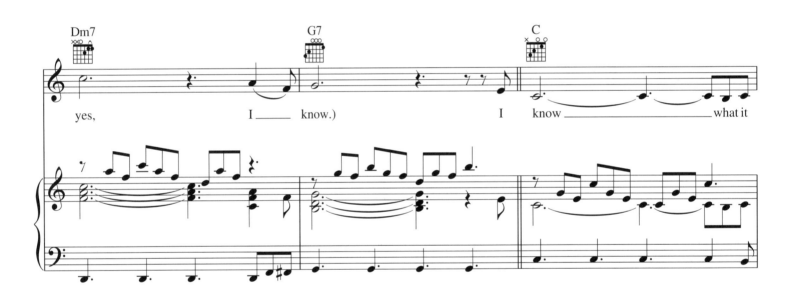

* *Recorded a half step lower.*

I LEFT MY HEART IN SAN FRANCISCO

Words by DOUGLASS CROSS
Music by GEORGE CORY

Moderate Waltz

The love - li - ness of Par - is seems some - how sad - ly gay. _____ The glo - ry

86

87

I WANNA BE AROUND

Words and Music by JOHNNY MERCER
and SADIE VIMMERSTEDT

I WILL WAIT FOR YOU

from THE UMBRELLAS OF CHERBOURG

Music by MICHEL LEGRAND
Original French Text by JACQUES DEMY
English Words by NORMAN GIMBEL

I'LL NEVER FALL IN LOVE AGAIN

from PROMISES, PROMISES

Lyric by HAL DAVID
Music by BURT BACHARACH

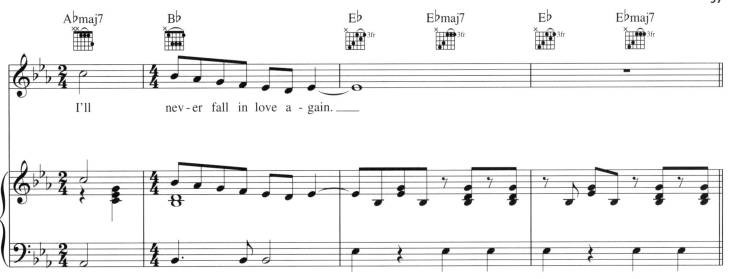

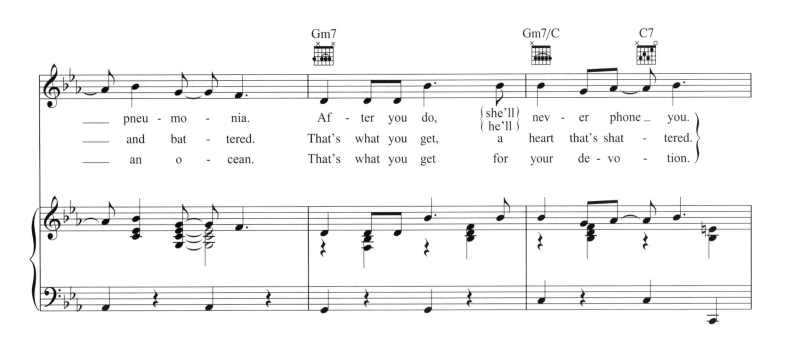

100

LIKE YOUNG

By ANDRE PREVIN
and PAUL FRANCIS WEBSTER

I'm out do- in' the u- su- al plac- es,
{She}
{He} goes where all the an- gry young men go,

and I'm liv- in' it like _____ young.
re- cites po- et- ry like _____ young.

THE IMPOSSIBLE DREAM
(The Quest)
from MAN OF LA MANCHA

Lyric by JOE DARION
Music by MITCH LEIGH

KING OF THE ROAD

Words and Music by
ROGER MILLER

A LITTLE BITTY TEAR

Words and Music by
HANK COCHRAN

LITTLE GREEN APPLES

Words and Music by
BOBBY RUSSELL

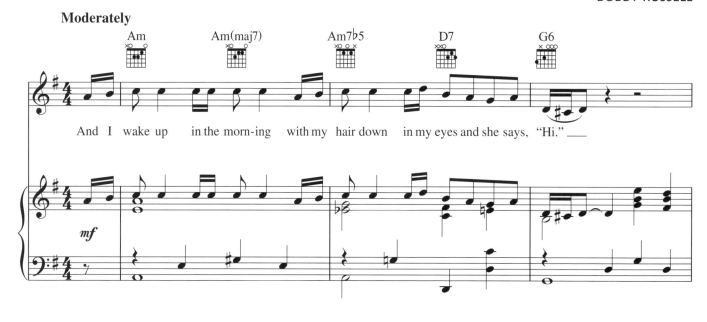

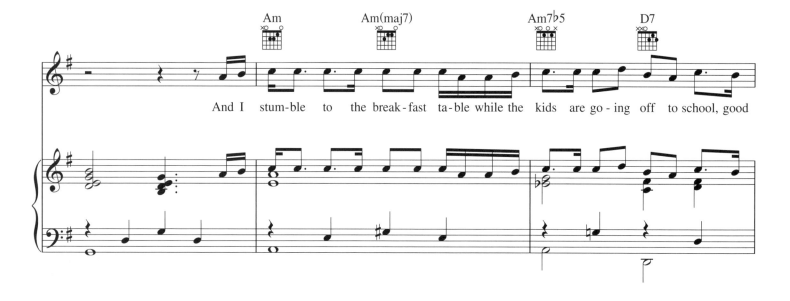

LOLLIPOPS AND ROSES

Words and Music by
TONY VELONA

MAKE SOMEONE HAPPY

from DO RE MI

Words by BETTY COMDEN and ADOLPH GREEN
Music by JULE STYNE

123

124

MOON RIVER

from the Paramount Picture BREAKFAST AT TIFFANY'S

Words by JOHNNY MERCER
Music by HENRY MANCINI

MICHELLE

Words and Music by JOHN LENNON
and PAUL McCARTNEY

MRS. ROBINSON
from THE GRADUATE

Words and Music by
PAUL SIMON

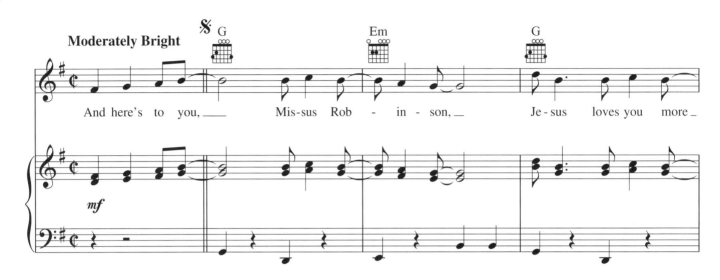

And here's to you, ___ Mis-sus Rob - in - son, ___ Je-sus loves you more ___

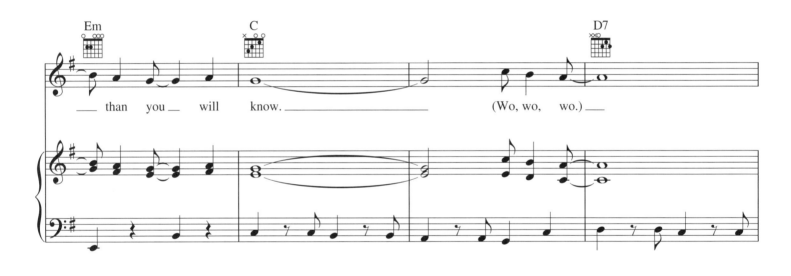

___ than you ___ will know. _____ (Wo, wo, wo.) ___

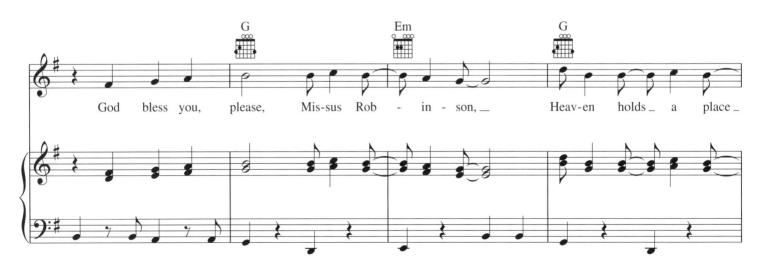

God bless you, please, Mis-sus Rob - in - son, ___ Heav-en holds _ a place _

MY COLORING BOOK

Words and Music by FRED EBB
and JOHN KANDER

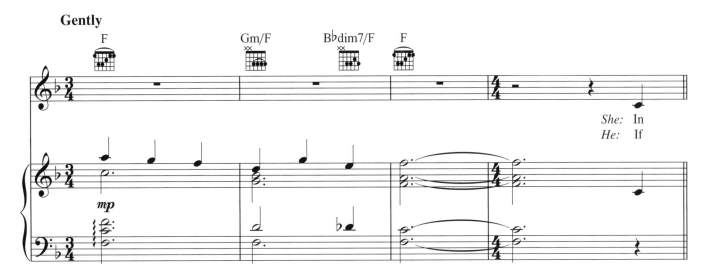

Gently

She: In
He: If

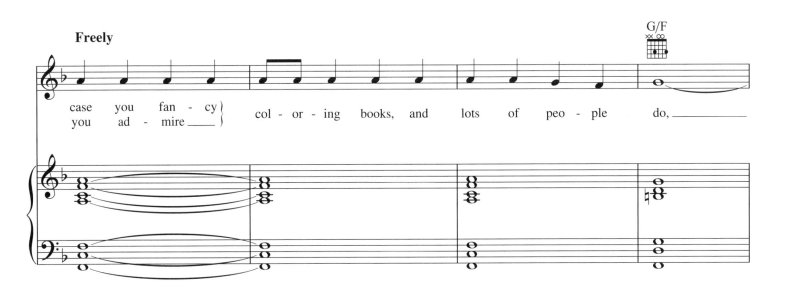

Freely

case you fan-cy
you ad-mire

col-or-ing books, and lots of peo-ple do, _____

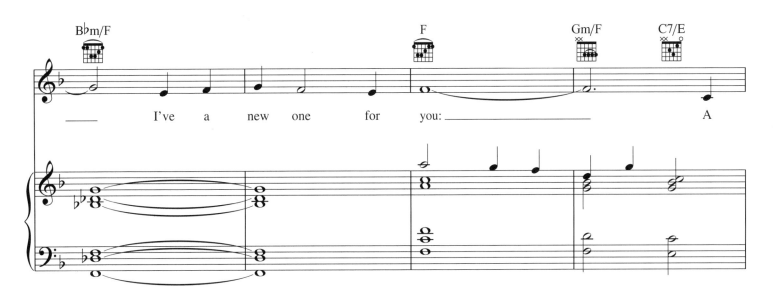

_____ I've a new one for you: _____ A

MY CUP RUNNETH OVER

from I DO! I DO!

Words by TOM JONES
Music by HARVEY SCHMIDT

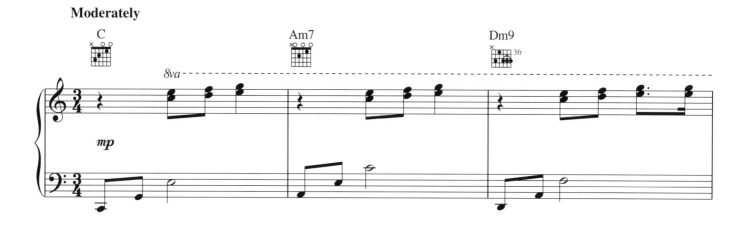

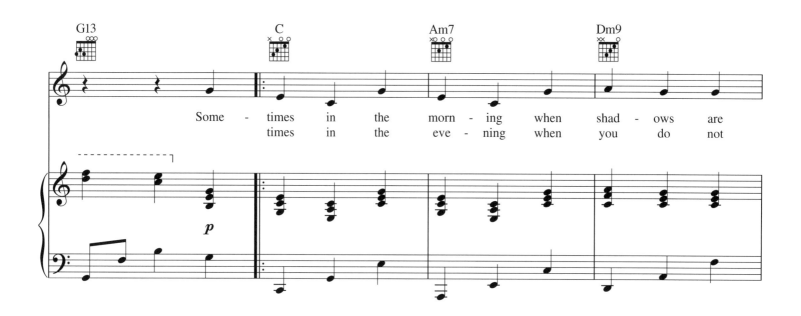

Some - times in the morn - ing when shad - ows are
times in the eve - ning when you do not

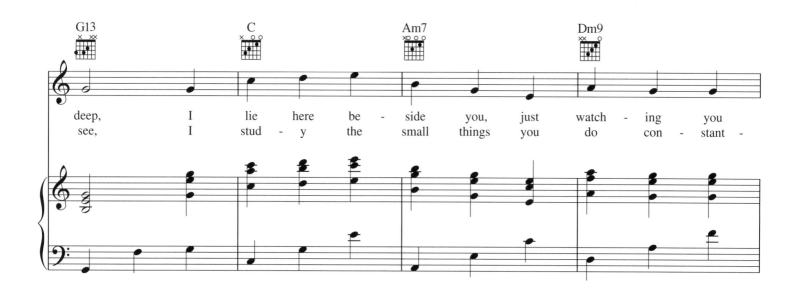

deep, I lie here be - side you, just watch - ing you
see, I stud - y the small things you do con - stant -

NICE 'N' EASY

Words and Music by LEW SPENCE,
ALAN BERGMAN and MARILYN BERGMAN

ODE TO BILLY JOE

Words and Music by
BOBBIE GENTRY

With a beat

1. It was the third of June, an-oth-er

2.-5. *(See additional lyrics)*

sleep-y, dust-y del-ta day, _____ I was

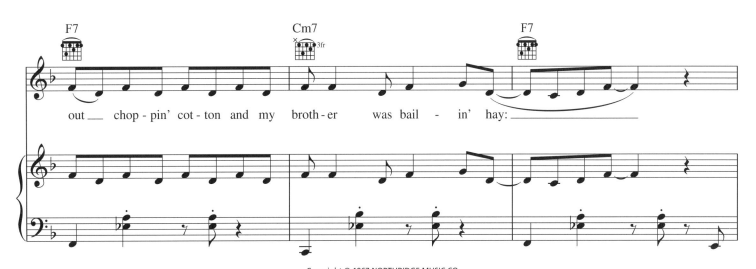

out __ chop-pin' cot-ton and my broth-er was bail-in' hay: _____

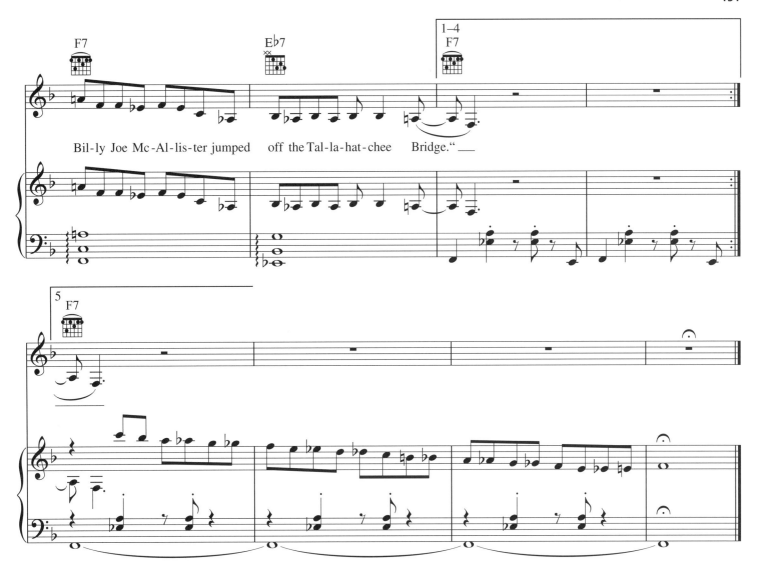

Bil-ly Joe Mc-Al-lis-ter jumped off the Tal-la-hat-chee Bridge." __

Additional Lyrics

2. Papa said to Mama, as he passed around the black-eyed peas,
"Well, Billy Joe never had a lick o' sense, pass the biscuits, please.
There's five more acres in the lower forty I've got to plow,"
And Mama said it was a shame about Billy Joe anyhow.
Seems like nothin' ever comes to no good up on Choctaw Ridge,
And now Billy Joe McAllister's jumped off the Tallahatchee Bridge.

3. Brother said he recollected when he and Tom and Billy Joe
Put a frog down my back at the Carroll County picture show,
And wasn't talkin' to him after church last Sunday night,
I'll have another piece of apple pie, you know, it don't seem right.
I saw him at the sawmill yesterday on Choctaw Ridge,
And now you tell me Billy Joe's jumped off the Tallahatchee Bridge.

4. Mama said to me, "Child, what's happened to your appetite?
I been cookin' all mornin' and you haven't touched a single bite.
That nice young preacher Brother Taylor dropped by today,
Said he'd be pleased to have dinner on Sunday. Oh, by the way,
He said he saw a girl that looked a lot like you up on Choctaw Ridge
And she an' Billy Joe was throwin' somethin' off the Tallahatchee Bridge."

5. A year has come and gone since we heard the news 'bout Billy Joe,
Brother married Becky Thompson, they bought a store in Tupeolo.
There was a virus goin' 'round, Papa caught it and he died last spring,
And now Mama doesn't seem to want to do much of anything.
And me I spend a lot of time pickin' flowers up on Choctaw Ridge,
And drop them into the muddy water off the Tallahatchee Bridge.

PEOPLE
from FUNNY GIRL

Words by BOB MERRILL
Music by JULE STYNE

RAINDROPS KEEP FALLIN' ON MY HEAD

from BUTCH CASSIDY AND THE SUNDANCE KID

Lyric by HAL DAVID
Music by BURT BACHARACH

to greet me. Rain-drops keep fall-in' on my head, but that does-n't mean my eyes will soon be turn-in' red. Cry-in's not for me 'cause I'm nev-er gon-na stop the rain by com-plain-in'. Be-cause I'm free, noth-in's wor-ry-in' me.

THE SECOND TIME AROUND
from HIGH TIME

Lyric by SAMMY CAHN
Music by JAMES VAN HEUSEN

THE SEPTEMBER OF MY YEARS

Words by SAMMY CAHN
Music by JAMES VAN HEUSEN

THE SHADOW OF YOUR SMILE

Love Theme from THE SANDPIPER

Lyric by PAUL FRANCIS WEBSTER
Music by JOHNNY MANDEL

168

SMALL WORLD
from GYPSY

Words by STEPHEN SONDHEIM
Music by JULE STYNE

SOMEWHERE, MY LOVE
Lara's Theme from DOCTOR ZHIVAGO

Lyric by PAUL FRANCIS WEBSTER
Music by MAURICE JARRE

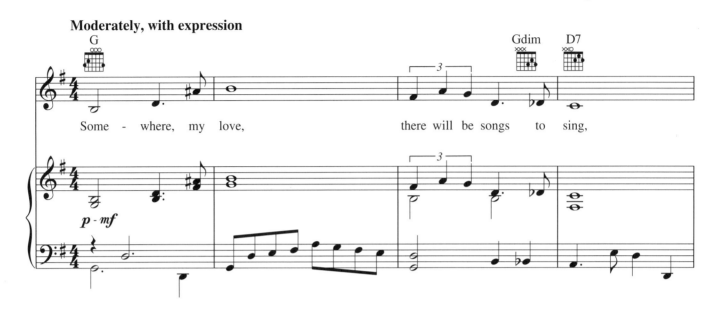

Some - where, my love, there will be songs to sing,

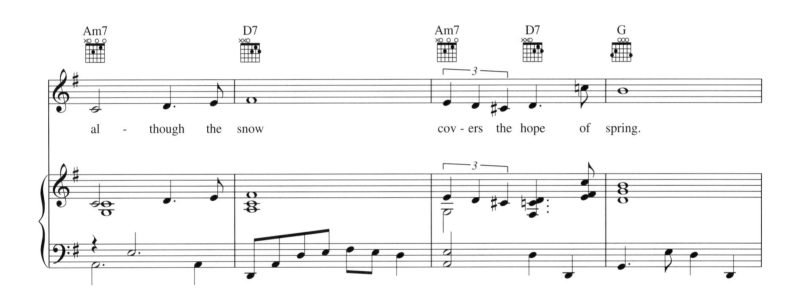

al - though the snow cov - ers the hope of spring.

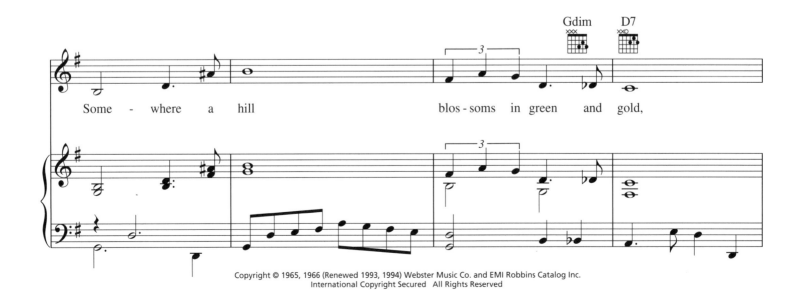

Some - where a hill blos - soms in green and gold,

STRANGERS IN THE NIGHT
adapted from A MAN COULD GET KILLED

Words by CHARLES SINGLETON and EDDIE SNYDER
Music by BERT KAEMPFERT

SPINNING WHEEL

Words and Music by
DAVID CLAYTON THOMAS

Moderately slow, with a beat

(Theme From)
A SUMMER PLACE
from A SUMMER PLACE

Words by MACK DISCANT
Music by MAX STEINER

Slowly

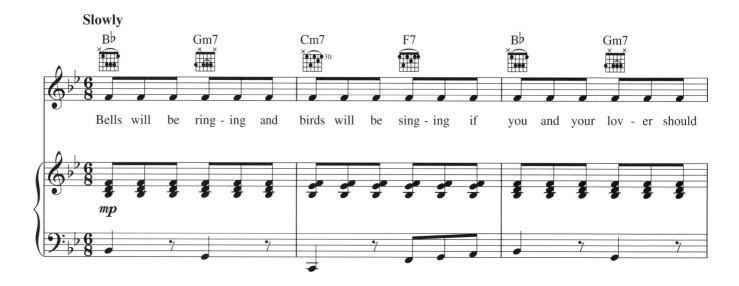

Bells will be ring-ing and birds will be sing-ing if you and your lov-er should

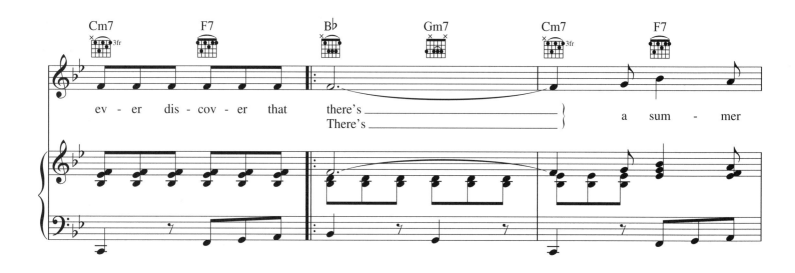

ev-er dis-cov-er that there's _____
There's _____ a sum-mer

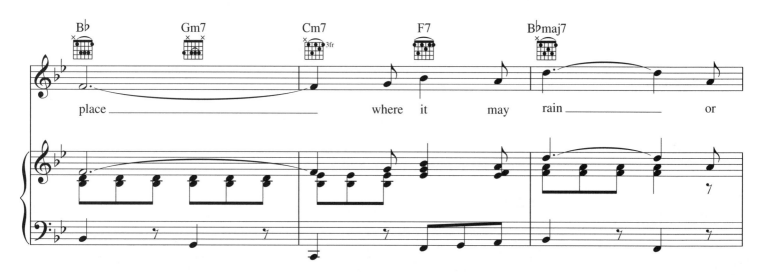

place _____ where it may rain _____ or

THE SWEETEST SOUNDS

from NO STRINGS

Lyrics and Music by
RICHARD RODGERS

Moderately

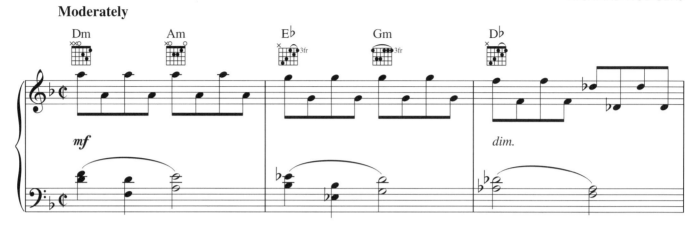

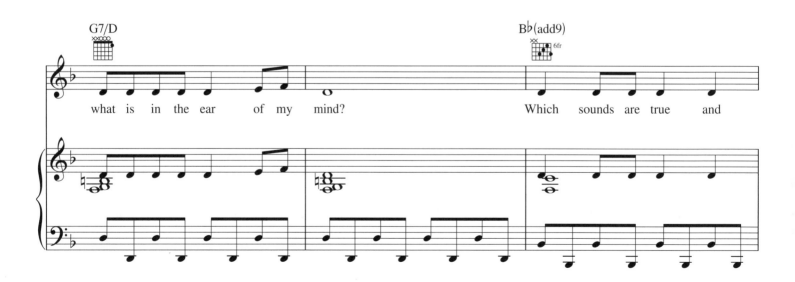

know Are wait - ing to be said. _____

_____ The most en - tranc - ing sight of

all is yet for me to see. _____

_____ And the dear - est love in all the

A TIME FOR US
(Love Theme)
from the Paramount Picture ROMEO AND JULIET

Words by LARRY KUSIK and EDDIE SNYDER
Music by NINO ROTA

VOLARE

Music by DOMENICO MODUGNO
Original Italian Text by D. MODUGNO and F. MIGLIACCI
English Lyric by MITCHELL PARISH

Some-times the world is a val-ley of heart-aches and tears,
Pen - so che un so - gno co - sì non ri - tor - ni mai più:

and in the hus-tle and bus-tle no sun-shine ap-
mi di - pin - ge - vo le ma - ni e la fac - cia di

oh! _____ No won-der my hap-py heart sings, your
oh! _____ *nel blu,* __ *di-pin-to di blu,* *fe-*

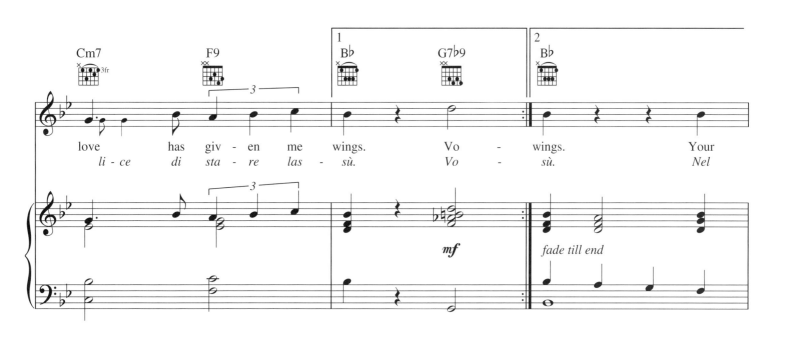

love has giv-en me wings. Vo - wings. Your
li - ce di sta - re las - sù. *Vo - sù.* *Nel*

love has giv-en me wings. Your love has giv-en me wings.
blu, di-pin-to di blu, *fe - li-ce di sta - re las - sù.*

UP, UP AND AWAY

Words and Music by
JIMMY WEBB

WHAT KIND OF FOOL AM I?

from the Musical Production STOP THE WORLD—I WANT TO GET OFF

Words and Music by LESLIE BRICUSSE
and ANTHONY NEWLEY

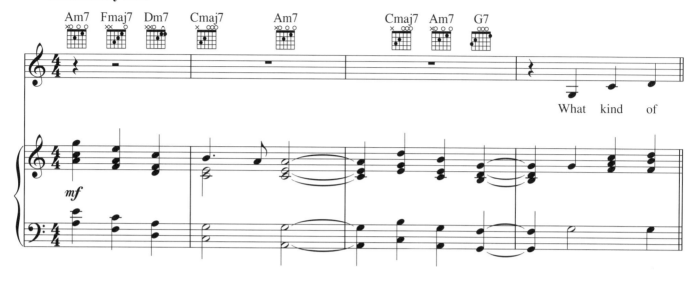

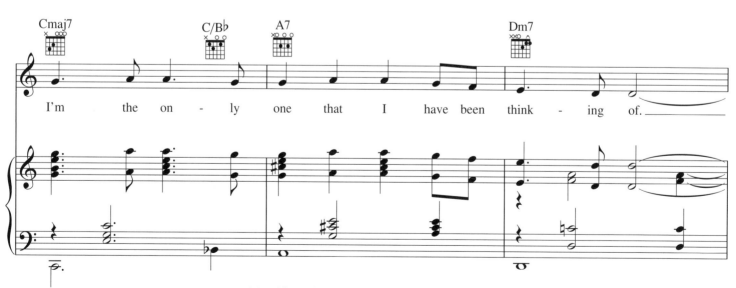

WHO CAN I TURN TO
(When Nobody Needs Me)
from THE ROAR OF THE GREASEPAINT – THE SMELL OF THE CROWD

Words & Music by LESLIE BRICUSSE
& ANTHONY NEWLEY

Slowly, with expression

Who can I turn to _____ when no-bod-y needs me? _____ My heart wants to know and so I must go where des-ti-ny leads me. _____

WITCHCRAFT

Music by CY COLEMAN
Lyrics by CAROLYN LEIGH

YESTERDAY

Words and Music by JOHN LENNON
and PAUL McCARTNEY

Moderately, with expression

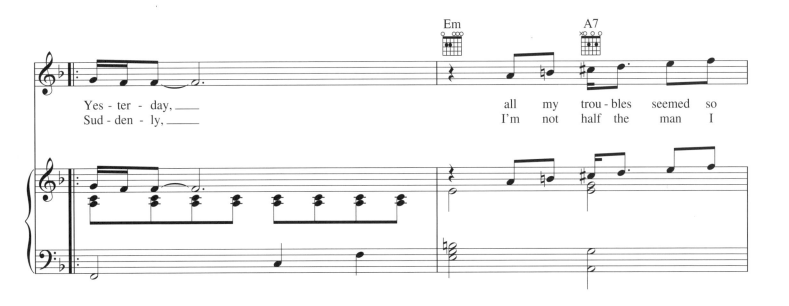

Yes - ter - day, ___ all my trou - bles seemed so
Sud - den - ly, ___ I'm not half the man I

far a - way, ___ now it looks as though ___ they're
used to be, ___ there's a shad - ow hang - ing

WIVES AND LOVERS

(Hey, Little Girl)

from the Paramount Picture WIVES AND LOVERS

Words by HAL DAVID
Music by BURT BACHARACH

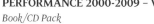